# Introduction to Succulents and Cacti

## Gardening Series

**Dueep Jyot Singh**

**Mendon Cottage Books**

*JD-Biz Publishing*

**Our books are available at:**

1. Amazon.com

2. Barnes and Noble

3. Itunes

4. Kobo

5. Smashwords

6. Google Play Books

# Table of Contents

# Introduction

The first time I heard the word "succulent" in reference to a group of plants, I was a bit bewildered. That was because I associated this particular term with delicious things to eat like succulent, juicy spareribs or succulent luscious fruit, fresh off a tree! But here was an experienced gardener talking about a plant, which he called a succulent? It did not look remotely edible at all!

Cacti belong to the "Succulent Plants" family. Plants with green leaves that are left in the sun without water are going to flag and wilt within a few hours. They are going to die within a few days. However, mother nature has made some plant equivalents of camels, which can go for long periods without any water.

These plants normally live in a hot and dry climate and they have managed to survive since the dawn of time. That is because they are able to adapt themselves to their environment. They are going to pass the dry season as leafless shrubs, seeds or as dry bulbs.

Cactus as well as other succulent plants are capable of storing moisture, in their stems and leaves, especially when there is plenty of moisture in the atmosphere. This is so that they can get plenty of liquid available to them, when the atmosphere becomes dry and arid.

**Since the smallest surface area for a given volume is a sphere, succulent plants are often spherical in shape. In fact, many of the cacti are of this form, at least when they are young.**

Succulent plants are normally found in areas, which are either semi-or completely desert areas. In a given period of time you are going to get long periods of drought and short periods of rain and cold. When the rain falls, the plant tissues are going to swell up. The moisture is going to be retained in the plant if it has adapted itself to prevent evaporation. This adaption is normally done by a protective covering, such as a layer of hair or wax or by a reduction of the surface area. These plants are also going to flower during the rainy season.

The stem is going to be swollen , but they are no leaves or perhaps you may see a few small leaves, when the growth begins every year. These are soon going to fall.

## How to Recognize Succulents

In an ordinary green plant, the leaves are going to contain a green substance which is known as chlorophyll. The plant is going to make use of the various food materials taken in by the roots in the presence of sunlight with the help of this chlorophyll.

However, when leaves are absent as in the case of succulents and cactuses, the same have to take over this particular function. That is the reason why stem succulents are normally going to have a lot of chlorophyll content, which means that they are normally green. However, as time goes by, the plant stem area near to the soil begins to turn yellowish – brown and wood like.

**Conophytum**

In many plants water is stored away in the leaves, which in extreme cases are going to become spherical in shape. But as in the case of Conophytum, a pair of leaves may be joined so closely into a body which is shaped like a top that just a small slit on the top of the body is going to indicate the dual origin.

# Conophytum

In a leaf succulent, the stem is often going to be much more reduced. The leaves are going to be crowded together to form a rosette. An advantage of this formation is that the overlapping leaves are going to prevent each other and also the soil below from drying out rapidly.

Apart from the plants in which water storage is definitely in a stem or a leaf, there are a number of plants where both stem and leaves are slightly succulent. Most of them are going to show surface adaptions which add to their attractive and decorative qualities.

Succulent plants are normally found in areas, where either there is a drought, or there is a chance of a drought because of the "salty" sand and soil.

I thought succulents were found only in desert areas, but I have also seen them in marshy lands, especially salt marshes. The succulents of course cannot absorb all the moisture that they required through the roots. That is because the salt content in the water is very high. The same thing occurs in cold regions with the low-temperature prevents the absorption of water. Still, brave hearts like *Sempervivum* managed to grow and survive in such harsh conditions.

It is just bad nomenclature that the name "cactus" is given to succulent plants, even though some may not belong to the cactus family. That is because their need for watering, is totally different from true cactuses and may be required at a different time of the year.

A true desert Cactus is not difficult to recognize. They are all stem succulents without leaves and generally with spines which arise from special organs known as *"areoles."* These are normally small protuberances arranged regularly on the surface of the plant. These generally bear hair as well as a number of spines. The spines in the center of an areole are going to differ from radial ones and they are characteristic of the plant. That is why a cactus is often identified by the spines when there are no flowers present.

Sometimes cactuses are confused with Euphorbias, which also have round and columnar stems without any leaves. When the spines are present on

Euphorbia plants – Spurges – they are not going to arise from areoles. They are going to appear in pairs or singly at regular positions up the ribs of the stem.

There are still other types of cactus from tropical forests. These are known as epiphytic cacti. That is because they grow on trees. These have thinner and slender stems in some species, the stems are flattened, but in these plants, though the spines are not well developed, they are going to come from small areoles often in "crenations" along the edge of the stems.

These type of cactuses are called leaf cactuses. Even though the name is misleading because although they have an appearance of being leaf like, the plants are going to consist of leafless stems.

# Cultivation of Cactuses

Cacti and others succulents are not difficult to grow, if the reason for their unusual form is remembered. They need an alternation of wet and dry periods because that is the sort of climate and atmosphere they are accustomed to in their native habitat. And naturally, they are going to prefer these particular changes of season at the correct time of the year depending on their land of origin.

True desert cacti are not going to be watered from October to March. During this period, you're going to allow them to rest. Many of them are going to stand and some of them even prefer a cooler temperature when they are resting but you need to protect them from frost.

**This is all very well outside in the desert, but don't let this happen to the cactus in your gardens.**

Plants with succulent leaves and much reduced stems neither definite resting time of some weeks or months. This resting time cannot necessarily be in the winter. Many succulents from South Africa or Australia where the seasons are reversed from other parts of the world may prefer to grow during winters and rest in summers. So look at your geographical location and then decide whether your cactus wants/needs watering or not.

Semi succulents which are plants with both the stems and leaves, slightly succulent, do not need such a definite period of rest but they prefer less water given to them after they have flowered.

Cacti are accommodating plants and that is why they can be kept in the greenhouse, living room, frame, or even out-of-doors. They however need plenty of light because after all, many of their ancestors survived in desert areas where the sun beat down upon their hardy heads for centuries.

If you're growing them in the living room, keep them as near to the window as possible. Also give them some ventilation if they are in the hot sun or there is a risk of their burning. You can stand the individual pots on a saucer or in an ornamental pot containing a bit of gravel or some granite chips. This is so that the pot does not remain standing in any excess of water that has run through after you have done the watering.

Remember to turn the pots occasionally. Otherwise the plants are going to be drawn towards any source of light and their shapes are going to be spoilt. You don't want lopsided succulents or cactus, do you. If your area is subject to a long dry spell, do put your cactus outside by all means. They enjoy the sun more than they would enjoy a long wet spell. Bring them back into the house or keep them under glass, if it starts to rain.

## Potting

Succulent plants are generally grown in pots, which may either be the normal traditional porous clay type or you may also use the plastic containers. In many ways plastic gives better results providing you realize that very much less amount of water is required since there is no evaporation through the sides of the plastic pot. Also, they are comparatively lighter to carry around from one place to another, especially if you have a number of cactus plants growing in a limited area. The only complaint I have against them is that they are not biodegradable!

Remember whether the pot is made up of clay or made up of plastic – it should have a drainage hole at the base. Cover this hole with broken crocks to prevent the soil from washing through whenever you water the plant.

The size of the pot should be such that the plant has sufficient space to grow, but it should not be too large. In such a case, the soil will remain too wet, if it is not penetrated by the roots in a few weeks.

# Best Potting Compost

We think that plants that live in the desert are not able to get the necessary nourishment in order to keep them healthy. That is not true. The soil is definitely not poor, though it may be sandy and loose. However, as there is not enough of rain to wash out the plant foods contained in the soil, this is going to be fairly rich in mineral salts

However, there is not going to be any humus, because after all that is available only in areas where there are trees and shrubs and the leaves are allowed to fall down annually or periodically and decompose. That is why desert cacti are not used to any sort of leaf mold. Do not put any leaf mold or very rich potting compost to the potting soil for such cacti.

**This rich soil may do well for flowering plants, but cacti prefer sandy soil.**

Your cacti are going to enjoy an open soil through which the water can drain rapidly. That means your cacti are going to flourish in a soil in which you have added some course and to the compost for more highly succulent plants. The best soil is going to be made of good loam, mixed with coarse sand.

## Re-Potting Your Cacti

If you have acquired the plants from a reliable source, you will not need to do any repotting for some time. However, you will have to do one test. Water your cacti. See if the soil has dried out in a few days. Turn the plant out and make sure that the roots are healthy and sound. That means they should look healthy and plump. If they are shriveled up, that means they are not healthy.

Disentangle the roots carefully. Remove any damaged portions. Repotting in fresh soil is going to give you a healthy cactus.

Young plants need to be repotted annually or as soon as you see that their roots are filling the pot. That means they need to be moved into a larger pot

Do not repot adult plants every year unless it is absolutely necessary, for the root tips through which the plants absorb the nourishment from the soil are going to be damaged during this process. The plant is thus going to receive a "shock" in consequence, and you may find your cactus not growing so happily in its new stylish, sunnier position.

If your cactus plant is really large, you definitely do not need to repot it. It is sufficient to remove the top layer of soil carefully and replace it with fresh soil, so that it can get even more of fresh nourishment.

# Watering of Your Succulents

Watering is a necessary and important operation and one which often presents great difficulties to beginners. You just need to remember that plants are going to become succulent only as a result of wet and dry periods. Naturally, these climactic factors are going to be maintained in cultivation of your succulents.

For very highly adapted plants which have very thick stems and leaves, the time of the year and the duration of the wet period is going to be very important. It should always coincide with the particular growing period of your plant.

The plants which you are growing in the greenhouse where heat and warmth is available in cold weather are going to be given the amount of water they need when they want it. But when you are growing the plants in a living room where the temperature and the ventilation is arranged to suit the human occupants, that is where you will need to do a little bit of compromising. That is why plants such as the desert cacti which need resting in winter are better grown in cooler conditions. So remove them if it is possible to an unheated room for the time of their rest. If they are kept in a living room, a little bit of water may be necessary to prevent the stems from shrinking away unduly.

The best way to learn how to water is to do a little bit of studying of the plant itself. Most of the plants may start growing whenever they wish to, whether they are watered or not. So as soon as you see a little bit of new growth appearing, give the plants some more water.

Once they have started growing freely, resume the normal watering procedure. A good water supply once a week is better than frequent showers and little dribbles of water. Remember never to give water to your succulents when the soil is still wet.

If a plant such as the desert cactus has been kept quite dry some time, you need to stand the pot in water until all the water soaks up to the surface. This means that the whole ball of soil is going to become evenly moist. Water semi-succulents throughout the year, but give them less water when they are not growing actively, usually after flowering.

# Propagation of Succulents

## Propagation through Seeds

Most of the succulent plants are easily raised from seed. And if you have obtained the seed from a reliable source, the plants are going to be true to type. Do not sow the seeds until about May, or the end of spring. You can also sow them earlier in especially constructed boxes, where the temperature is between 10 – 13°C [50 – 55°F.] Seeds which are sown in a higher temperature may germinate more rapidly, but the seedlings are going to find it difficult to grow on as time goes by.

Distribute the seed evenly over the surface of the soil. If the seeds are larger than small pinheads, cover them with a light sifting of the soil, as fine as you can make it.

Unless they are overcrowded, leave the small seedlings which are difficult to handle in that particular seed pan for a year. Wait till the next growing period arrives. Do not allow them to get dry. This is going to check the growth.

If there are number of seedlings prick them out together into one pan. This is going to help in keeping them moist instead of separating them in different pots. The moment when you find that their growth is satisfactory, you can remove them from their crowded seed pan and place them individually in their individual possibly permanent pots.

## Propagation through Cuttings

Another very popular method of propagation of succulents and cacti is by cuttings. When the side branches can be removed without spoiling the parent plant, you can root them separately. Break them off at the joint or cut neatly with a sharp knife. If the flesh is moist, leave the cut surfaces to dry for a day or two. That is before you put the cuttings in the cutting box where the rooting material is made up of a mixture of medium grade peat and fine sand. This is easy to keep moist.

If you are using a medium-sized box or a seed pan filled up with this mixture, you can put a number of cuttings of all types here. The mixture is going to keep in good condition for a number of months. All this while a succession of cuttings are going to be rooted in it, as space allows. Remember to label all the cuttings.

It is not necessary to cover the box with glass. This is what you normally do with the cuttings of soft leaved plants. That is because succulents are not going to wilt easily. Also, there is less danger of rot if there is plenty of air around them.

Never take the cuttings out of the potting soil to see how they are getting on. This is going to destroy the embryo roots. Wait for signs of growth at the top of the cutting before you lift them out carefully for re – potting purposes.

## Leaf cuttings

A number of succulent plants, such as *Echeverria, Crassula, and Haworthia* can be propagated from leaves. I remember doing this experiment for the first time in my life when I was about 10 years ago and this method of revocation had been shown to us students by our botany teacher. Soon all of us had succulent plant leaves planted in boxes, and we could see tiny plants coming out from their edges.

For this you just need to detach the leaves from the stem. Remember not to cut them off. Lay them in a mixture of peat and sand. The base of the leaf has to be covered. Water your leaf. You are soon going to see baby plants, developing from the leaf. Do not detach the old leaf until it has dried up completely. By then the new plant is going to be sufficiently rooted. You can now pot it separately.

## Propagation through Offsets

Some succulent plants are going to make offsets around the base of the plants. If these are left all alone, you can find a fine clump forming because this is a natural way in which such a plant grows in its natural habitat.

If extra plants are wanted, you can detach some of these offsets. And if you found that they have already made some roots, you can pot them immediately. However, if there are no roots, you can treat them as cuttings.

# Pests and Diseases

Succulent plants do not suffer greatly from pests. However, if you find any insects here, remove them at once with tweezers or you can just use a paint brush to brush them off.

The commonest pest which you are going to find on your cactus or on your succulents is a mealy bug. This is small and whitish in color. It is going to lay its eggs in cocoons which are normally going to resemble cotton wool. You can see both the insect and the eggs clearly.

It is difficult to get rid of these mealy bugs because they are covered with wax. That is why most insecticides are not capable of destroying them. That is why the only way which you can remove them is by brushing them off.

If you find these mealy bugs, around the roots, in the shape of white threads when you are repotting your plant, just put the roots underwater. Do this until all traces of the bugs are removed, then repot in fresh soil and in a clean pot.

You may also find scale insects on your succulents. Remove them immediately because they are going to suck all the juices from the stem, and they are going to damage the surface of the plant. The insect itself is quite soft. It is covered with a durable and "horny" shell. It clamps this shell down on the plant. The moment you remove the shell, the insect is going to die. Thanks to the durable shell, it is incapable of being affected with pesticides. So you can remove this particular pest with a blunt instrument.

There is one mite which is called red spider, even though it is not a spider. It is going to do considerable damage whenever it appears, especially as it is so small that it is rarely noticed and your plant is badly damaged.

It is usually going to occur on plants that have been kept in a very dry atmosphere or plants which have been grown in an over warm room. Overwatering can also produce this particular pest. Spray your plant with water. This is going to destroy the pest, but the disfiguring damage on your stem is going to remain.

# Diseases

Diseases are not common among well grown succulents and cactuses, but damage can be caused by an accident happening to the roots or the stem, which is going to set up rot in the tissue. In such a case, all you have to do is scrape the damaged part away. After that you need to treat the surface with the flowers of sulfur and the plant is going to heal.

"Flowers of sulfur" is a yellow powdery substance which is normally found in volcanic areas. For millenniums men have been using it as a fungicide as well as an insecticide. They have also been using it to cure skin diseases. So cure your injured cactus with this powder by sprinkling some flowers of sulfur on the damaged surface.

When the base of the plant has become rotten through excess water in the soil, you may find that the roots have suffered. Under such circumstances, you need to cut off the top of the plant above the portion which is rotten. Now treat the cut off portion with flowers of sulfur and re-root it again as a cutting.

# Cultivated Succulent Plants

### *Crassula sp.*

Succulent plants are normally classed together because they resemble each other in their adaptation to dry conditions. However, they do not all belong to the same plant family. There are 24 families in which some degree of succulence is going to be found, but only three of them – the Cactus, the Crassula, and the Mesembryanthemaceae families consist of plants where all the plants are succulent.

A large number of succulent plants are now grown all over the world, and if the generic or the first Latin name of the plant is known to you, you can get an idea of the type of the plant. You can also go to the nearest nursery and order it.

Remember that nobody can really be very certain about the flowering times of succulents or cactuses, because that is going to depend on the weather, the amount of sunshine the plant is going to get, and how well you take care of your plants. Other species in one particular genus may not flower at the same time, especially they come from different climates. This is going to happen in *Crassula*. There is no time in the year when none of the species is flowering and no two species are going to flower at the same time!

In succulents, it is the plant itself that is of chief importance. If flowers come, they are a welcome addition. But many of them are not going to flower regularly and some may never reach flowering stages in some countries, particularly where the weather is comparatively cooler and the sun does not shine every day.

My mother got obsessed with cactuses about two decades ago, and now the roof is covered with plenty of small, large and medium-sized cactuses of different varieties. And every time I visit that particular roof garden, I am surprised to see a flower peeking out from some plant which I – not totally obsessed with cactuses – considered to be just a small spherical lump of spiky green. But then I see the flower and say, "oh my, how lovely this is!" These flowers are quite capable of turning "supposed lumps of spiky green" into something really colorful, attractive, and very pleasing to the eye.

Similarly, it is impossible to predict the height of most succulents. I remember one of my colleagues bringing a baby Yucca – a true desert cactus – into the office and wanting to stand it in one corner of the office reception room. Now I knew that they could grow into real giant plants, so I asked that it be planted in a large container so that we did not have to shift it when it hit 6 feet. She was skeptical, because in her garden, none of the plants had grown up to more than 3 feet, and I did not want to tell her, "it is early days yet!"

Anyway, now that baby Yucca which has flourished inside the office for more than a decade is topping more than 6 feet, thanks to the loving care and attention being given to it and we give her triumphant "I told you so" looks. To which she shrugs her shoulder and says defensively, "how do I know that cactuses can grow so tall." Well, they do! Occasionally! Depending on the variety!

But when they are healthy, and good-looking, they are magnificent plants. When you cultivate them. You can find good representatives of the same plant, which are going to a widely in size according to their age and the conditions of cultivation. That is why if I give you the height that the plants can attain in their natural surroundings, this may be misleading because it is possible that you cannot replicate those particular conditions of temperature and soil.

Here are some popular varieties, which you may know and what you would want to plant in your garden –

## Agave

These are natives of America. The leaves are thick, usually tapering and sometimes with spiny edges. They are held in rosettes which are usually on short stems. When fully grown, most of them are extremely large plants but small specimens are very attractive and they grow slowly.

## Aloe

Anybody who is beauty conscious and into natural remedies for skin ailments and beautification, is going to recognize the word Aloe immediately. This is a succulent. These are natives of Africa. These plants vary in size. Some of them have stems; others do not have any stems. There are some species where the stem is going to increase in height and you may find aloe trees growing in their native land!

The leaves are thick and tapering sometimes with spiny edges. They are held in rosettes. The flowers are usually red or orange. They grow in winter and they require less water in summer. You can repot them in September.

Some of the aloe varieties which are very popular are *Aloe Vera, Aloe arborescens, Aloe aristata , Aloe variegata*, etc.

## Conophytum

These are "mimicry mesembryanthemums." Each pair of leaves are going to be joined so closely together that a small top shaped body with a slit across the upper surface is going to be formed. The surface may be flat, lobed, or curved. The flowers are going to emerge through the slits after which the plant is going to divide.

Keep the plants completely dry from December until June. By this time, the outer pair of the leaves are going to dry up to a papery skin. This is going to split when the growth begins. You have about 200 species in this particular genus.

## Crassula

This genus includes a wide variety of types which are found commonly in South and Southwest Africa. *Crassula arborescens* is a large shrub, *Crassula cooperii* forms mats of small rosettes of prettily marked leaves. *Crassula schmidtii* is made up of low branching stems with rosettes of leaves. The centers of the leaves are going to elongate into inflorescence bearing small red flowers.

## Echeveria

This is a genus native to America. This is a spring growing plant. The leaves are in rosettes. They are either stem less or on branching stems. As a rule, they are going to have a coating of wax or hair on the surface. This is going to make them very decorative. The flowers are red or orange in loose sprays.

# Euphorbia

This is a spring growing plant.

This genus is worldwide in its distribution. Only a few of the species are succulent. Some are from South Africa. They are often mistaken for cacti because of their columnar and spiny stems, but they belong to another distinct family as can be seen by their flowers, which are quite small and insignificant.

A milky juice/latex exudes out if the skin of the plant is broken. In many cases it is poisonous. That is why the moment we touched Euphorbias, when we were children – being real stubborn spoilt brats we needed to go and see the latex even though the plant was dangerous – we were immediately told to wash our hands with cold water and salt, many many times. Unless, of course, we wanted to be blinded with the poisonous milk. This was going to happen if we managed to get some of that poison into our eyes when we rubbed our eyes with those hands.

That brought us to our senses, and even today, I do not approach a Euphorbia, if I can help it.

## Haworthia

These are spring plants and the genus is from South and Southwest Africa. It is related to the aloes but the plants are smaller. The leaves are in rosettes and the small white flowers are held in a long loose inflorescence.

These plants grow mostly in the winter and need less of water in the summer. You can repot them in September. Many of these plants have thick skin and grow well in the sun.

## Opuntia

This is a very large group of cacti found all over America. However, the types are going to differ in different areas. The stems are jointed and the joints may be flattened, globular in shape or cylindrical. The spines vary in number and type.

The characteristic of this particular genus is that there are going to be bristles which are barbed. These are produced in each areole. They are called glochids.

If you like Westerns, you may have often read comic scenes in which the villain or the clownish sidekick falls into an Opuntia and comes out as spiny as a porcupine and yowling like a coyote. This is because these spines get detached easily. So if you find yourself with these barbed spines under your skin, you can remove them by pressing adhesive plaster down over them. After that you need to peel off that plaster carefully and it is going to remove the spine.

Most of these Opuntias do not flower freely when they are cultivated.

Apart from these popular succulents and cacti, there are other cacti genus and varieties, including *Kalanchoe,Faucaria, Epiphyllum, Gasteria,Litho* , etc.

## Mesembryanthemums- Fenestraria

These are summer plants. They are also called as window plants in many parts of the world.(From Fenestre- old French word for "window".) The upper surface of the leaves is translucent. They are cylindrical in shape. There also held in rosettes. Basically, they are shrubby types, native to South and Southwest Africa.

# Conclusion

This book has given you plenty of knowledge about succulents and cacti. Not only are they going to add that touch of class and distinction to your garden, but they are also going to flourish for years if they have plenty of spreading space.

In many parts of these, cacti are considered unworthy plants to plant in gardens. That is because there is a medieval superstition about them that a house in which a cactus grows is going to be a house of strife, quarrels, disputes and disharmony. I can see the psychological basis behind such an idea, and there is justified reason for such a belief. For millenniums the East has been made up of joint families. Just imagine that one particular family member has a favorite cactus growing in one corner of the garden. And another family member with whom relations are not so cordial has a pack of children.

One fine day one adventurous child is definitely going to fiddle around with the cactus plant and get spikes into him. When he comes crying home to his mama, she is going to take up arms in righteous indignation and go kick up a donnybrook with the owner of the cactus.

The proud owner is definitely going to defend himself and tell the female to take better care of her curious offspring, making sure that it does not go wandering around places where cacti grow. And matters are going to escalate. So that is the reason why these plants were never grown in Eastern Gardens.

When I told my mother about this particular superstition, and the reason behind it, she said, well, she had grown up children and nearly grown-up grandchildren and none of them were going to come investigating her cacti out of sheer imbecility! So she was going to enjoy them thoroughly!

Talking about mesembryanthemums. These come under some of my favorite succulents because I can just plant them in my garden and forget to water them. They are going to flourish as long as they can grow in the shade and have plenty of available space to spread themselves high and wide. They are amazingly attractive basket plants. And they do not bother much about the weather. As long as they get a little bit of water every 6 to 8 days, they are going to gladden everybody's hearts.

Anyway, I remember an enthusiastic (and adult) family member drowning these succulent plants, because according to him they were green and flowering. How could they be desert plants? How could they be succulents? Well, that is one thing you need to explain to newbies. So, well, when I came back from my official tour, after a month my poor little anthemums' had drowned due to overwatering and waterlogging.[1]

After I stopped screaming, – because I had got them from the mountains during a weekend and they were the envy of the neighborhood – I decided to check in my favorite nursery whether they had these plants.

The nursery man could not recognize them by my description of light green leaves with dark Crimson flowers and kept asking me to bring him a plant so that he could recognize it and give me what I wanted. I was not going to the mountains just to pick up my favorite plants to show to a perplexed nursery gardener! So I told him that it was a mesembryanthemum. He could just show me his collection of mesembryanthemums and I could recognize my favorite plant.

He swallowed. And then he said in a small voice – Are you sure, that you have got the plant's name correct? Yep, I said, in a bewildered tone. He explained hurriedly. Actually, everybody in the city called them "mesemanthebrums" and were they what I wanted?

"All right, just lead me to your mesemanthebrums, Macduff", said I, and managed to find my particular variety of whatever it is called! And it is now flourishing in three huge hanging window baskets on my terrace. All from

---

[1] Reminds me about one of the incidents in the lives and times of the well-known world famous naturalist Gerald Durrell. He left some baby hedgehogs in the keeping of his sister Margo, with a list of the amount of food they needed to be given throughout the day. He came back after a couple of months and found those baby hedgehogs dead. She being a caring lady could not bear to see them looking so hungry and she had over- fed them to death! Ah well, killing with kindness and through the best of intentions – plants and animals – comes instinctively to a number of us human beings!

one plant cutting. So remember with a little bit of love and care, your succulents are going to spread their wings and grow.

Live Long and Prosper!

# Author Bio

**Dueep Jyot Singh** is a Management and IT Professional who managed to gather Postgraduate qualifications in Management and English and Degrees in Science, French and Education while pursuing different enjoyable career options like being an hospital administrator, IT,SEO and HRD Database Manager/ trainer, movie , radio and TV scriptwriter, theatre artiste and public speaker, lecturer in French, Marketing and Advertising, ex-Editor of Hearts On Fire (now known as Solstice) Books Missouri USA, advice columnist and cartoonist, publisher and Aviation School trainer, ex-moderator on Medico.in, banker, student councilor ,travelogue writer … among other things!

One fine morning, she decided that she had enough of killing herself by Degrees and went back to her first love—writing. It's more enjoyable! She already has 48 published academic and 14 fiction- in- different- genre books under her belt.

When she is not designing websites or making Graphic design illustrations for clients , she is browsing through old bookshops hunting for treasures, of which she has an enviable collection – including R.L. Stevenson, O.Henry, Dornford Yates, Maurice Walsh, De Maupassant, Victor Hugo, Sapper, C.N. Williamson, "Bartimeus" and the crown of her collection- Dickens "The Old Curiosity Shop," and "Martin Chuzzlewit" and so on… Just call her "Renaissance Woman" ) - collecting herbal remedies, acting like Universal Helping Hand/Agony Aunt, or escaping to her dear mountains for a bit of exploring, collecting herbs and plants and trekking.

Check out some of the other JD-Biz Publishing books

Gardening Series on Amazon

# Health Learning Series

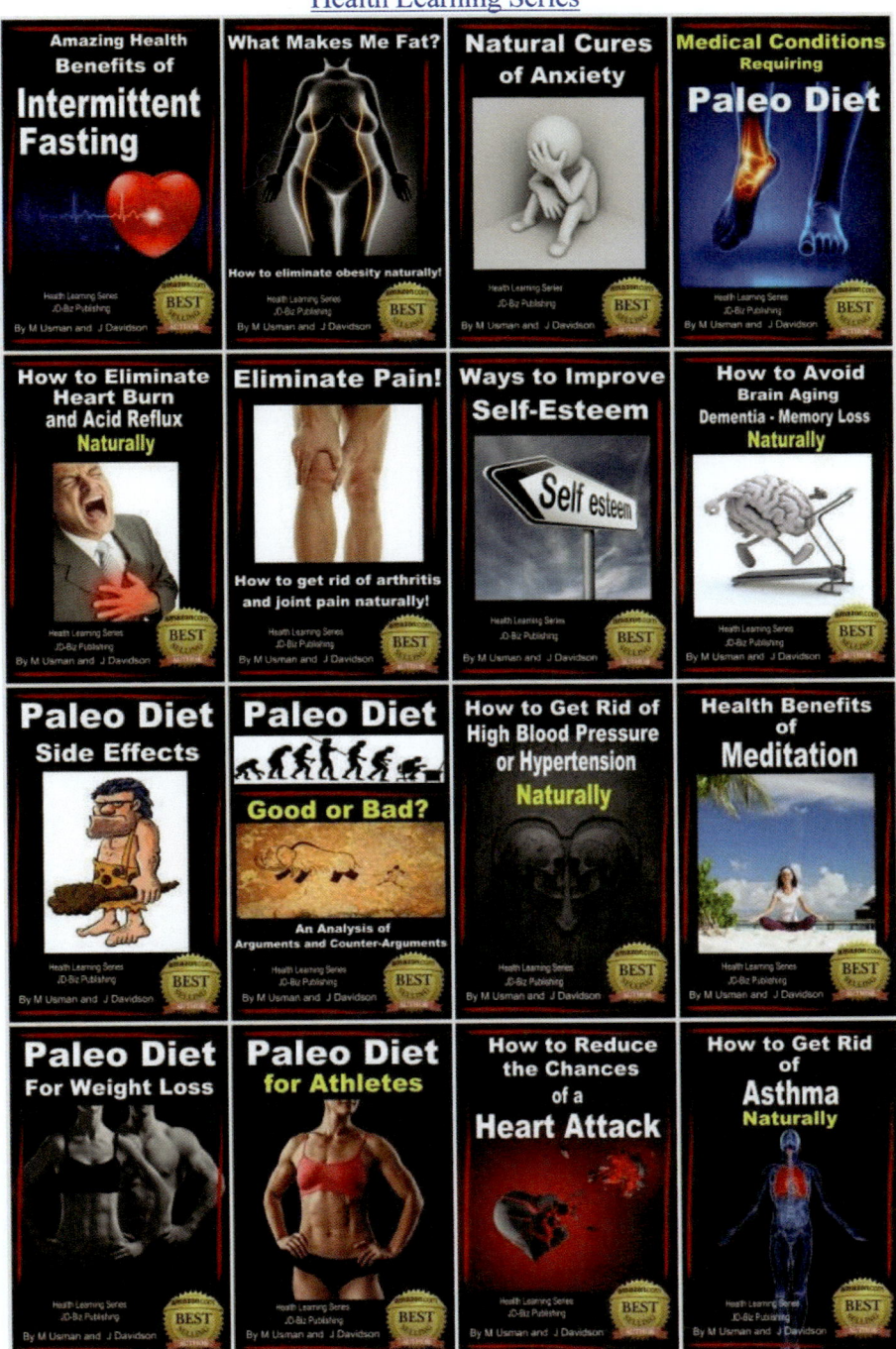

## Amazing Animal Book Series

# Learn To Draw Series

## How to Build and Plan Books

## Entrepreneur Book Series

Our books are available at

1. [Amazon.com](Amazon.com)

2. [Barnes and Noble](Barnes and Noble)

3. [Itunes](Itunes)

4. [Kobo](Kobo)

5. [Smashwords](Smashwords)

6. [Google Play Books](Google Play Books)

# Publisher

JD-Biz Corp

P O Box 374

Mendon, Utah 84325

http://www.jd-biz.com/

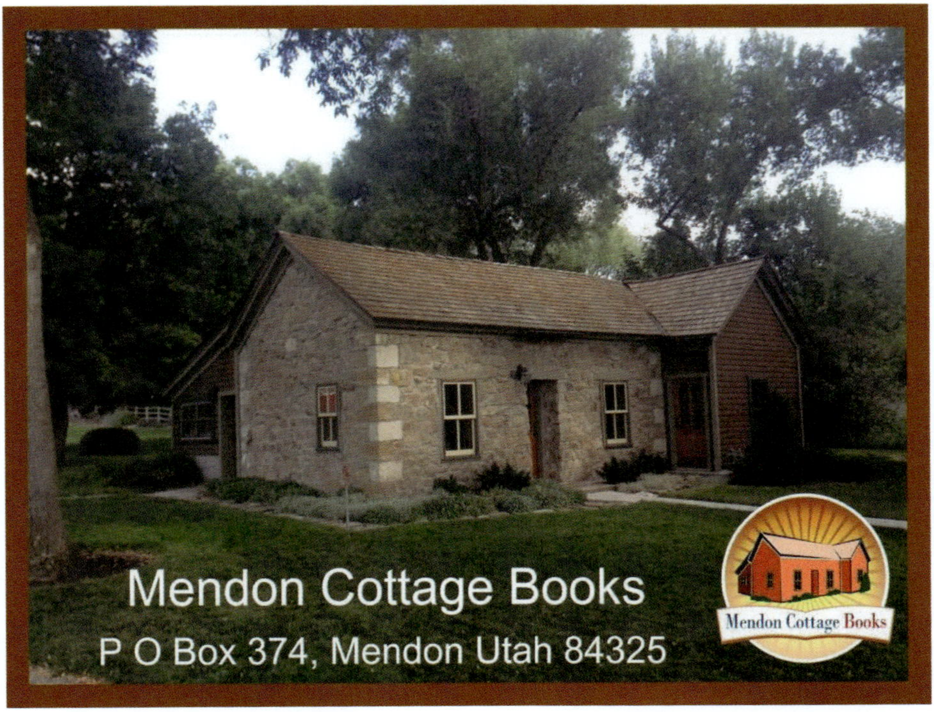

Mendon Cottage Books

P O Box 374, Mendon Utah 84325

Printed in Great Britain
by Amazon